Torque brims with excitement perfect for thrill-seekers of all kinds. Discover daring survival skills, explore uncharted worlds, and marvel at mighty engines and extreme sports. In *Torque* books, anything can happen. Are you ready?

This edition first published in 2024 by Bellwether Media, Inc.

No part of this publication may be reproduced in whole or in part without written permission of the publisher. For information regarding permission, write to Bellwether Media, Inc., Attention: Permissions Department, 6012 Blue Circle Drive, Minnetonka, MN 55343.

Library of Congress Cataloging-in-Publication Data

Names: McKinney, Donna, author.
Title: F-22 Raptor / by Donna McKinney.
Description: Minneapolis, MN : Bellwether Media, Inc., 2024. |
 Series: Torque: Military Aircraft | Includes bibliographical references and
 index. | Audience: Ages 5-8 | Audience: Grades 4-6 | Summary: "Engaging
 images accompany information about the F-22 Raptor. The combination of
 high-interest subject matter and light text is intended for students in
 grades 3 through 7" – Provided by publisher.
Identifiers: LCCN 2023046953 (print) | LCCN 2023046954 (ebook) |
 ISBN 9798886878196 (library binding) | ISBN 9798886879131 (ebook)
Subjects: LCSH: F-22 (Jet fighter plane)–Juvenile literature. |
 United States. Air Force–Juvenile literature.
Classification: LCC UG1242.F5 M3978 2024 (print) | LCC UG1242.F5 (ebook) |
 DDC 358.4/383–dc23/eng/20231019
LC record available at https://lccn.loc.gov/2023046953
LC ebook record available at https://lccn.loc.gov/2023046954

Text copyright © 2024 by Bellwether Media, Inc. TORQUE and associated logos are trademarks and/or registered trademarks of Bellwether Media, Inc.

Editor: Kieran Downs   Designer: Jeffrey Kollock

Printed in the United States of America, North Mankato, MN.

TABLE OF CONTENTS

MOVING AT SUPERSONIC SPEED	4
WHAT IS THE F-22 RAPTOR?	6
BUILT TO WIN	10
THE RAPTOR'S FUTURE	18
F-22 RAPTOR FACTS	20
GLOSSARY	22
TO LEARN MORE	23
INDEX	24

MOVING AT SUPERSONIC SPEED

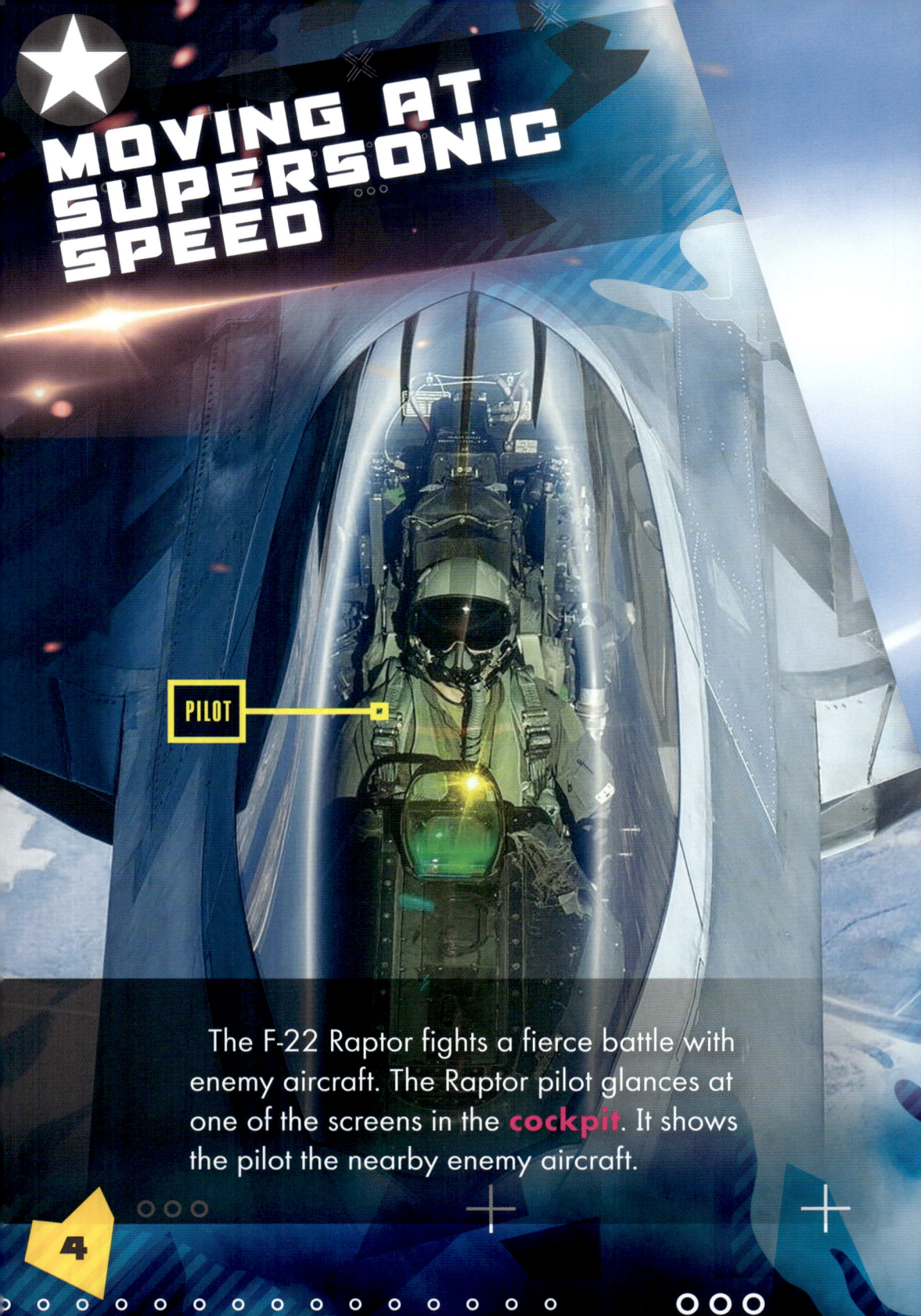

PILOT

The F-22 Raptor fights a fierce battle with enemy aircraft. The Raptor pilot glances at one of the screens in the **cockpit**. It shows the pilot the nearby enemy aircraft.

4

But enemy pilots cannot catch the Raptor. The pilot turns on the **afterburner**. The Raptor flies through the air at **supersonic** speed. Its powerful engines carry it to safety!

WHAT IS THE F-22 RAPTOR?

The F-22 Raptor is one of the top fighter jets in the United States Air Force. It is built to battle enemies in the air and on the ground.

The Raptor is fast and **agile**. Its **stealth** technology helps it hide from enemies. Its weapons make it powerful in battle.

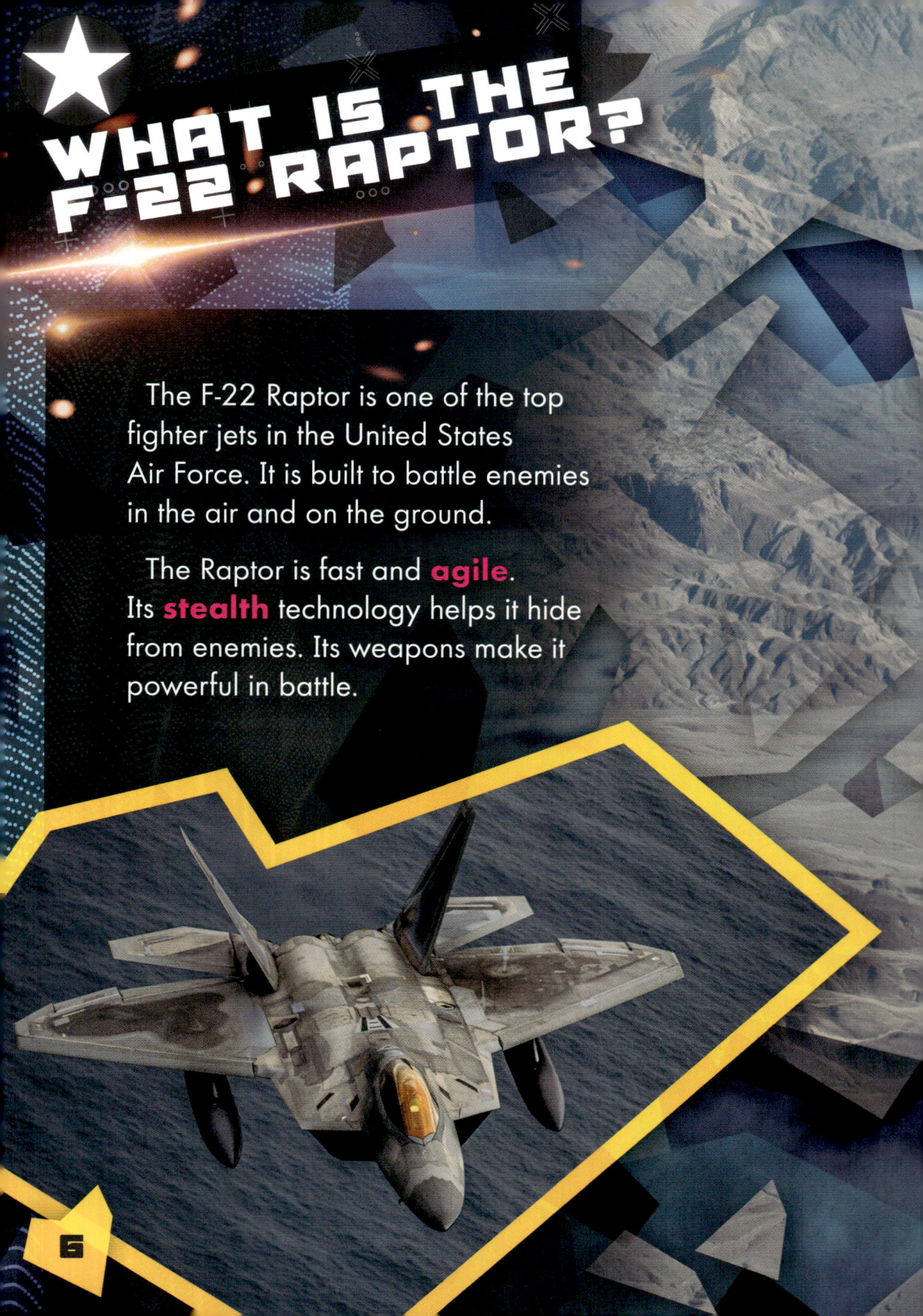

EYES ON THE ENEMY

The Raptor can be powerful in battle. But its work also includes spying on enemies!

The first Raptors were built in 1997. The U.S. Air Force began flying Raptors in 2005. The Raptor replaced the F-15 Eagle.

F-15 EAGLE

The Raptor flew its first **combat** missions in Syria in 2014. In 2023, a Raptor shot down a Chinese balloon over the U.S. The U.S. military believed it was a spy balloon.

MISSIONS MAP

	Shot down an unidentified "object"	Alaska, 2023
	Fought against the Islamic State of Iraq and Syria (ISIS)	Syria, 2014
	Shot down a Chinese spy balloon	near the coast of South Carolina, 2023

BUILT TO WIN

The Raptor was built to be the best fighter in the air. The Air Force wanted an aircraft that could defeat all other enemy fighter jets in the world.

PARTS OF AN
F-22 ⊙ RAPTOR

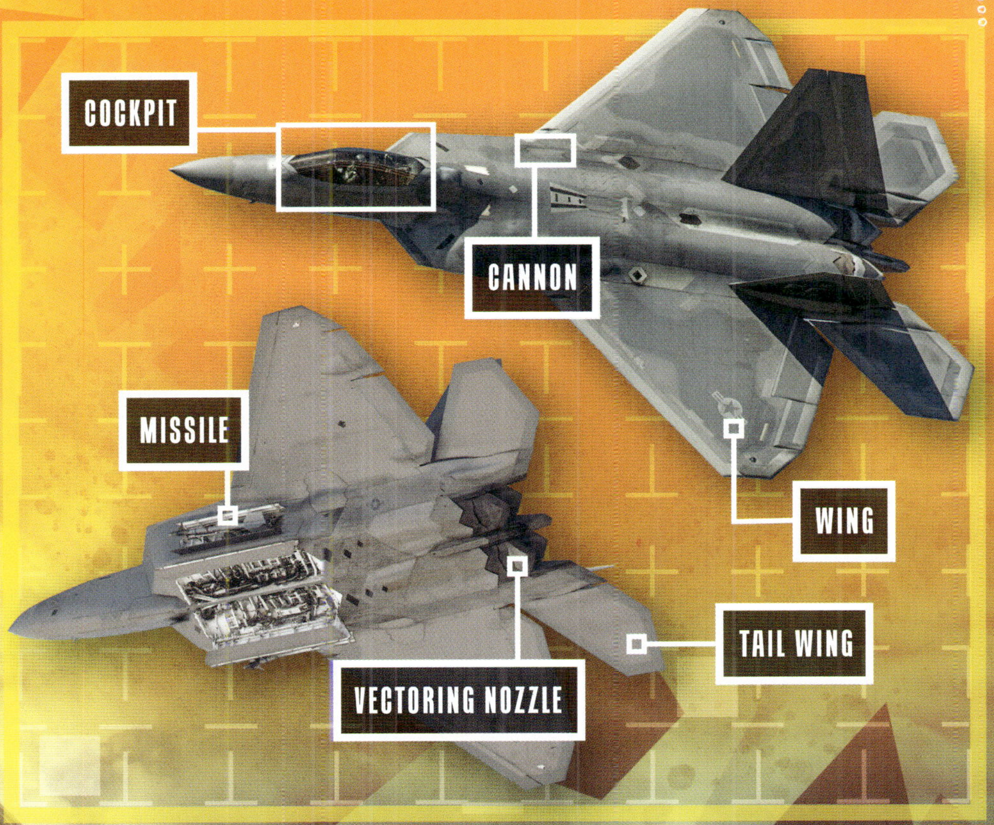

- COCKPIT
- CANNON
- MISSILE
- WING
- TAIL WING
- VECTORING NOZZLE

The U.S. is the only military to fly F-22s. The U.S. does not want the special technology in the F-22 to fall into the hands of its enemies.

The Raptor can move better than any other fighter aircraft. Its **thrust vectoring** allows for it to make sharp turns at high speeds.

THRUST VECTORING

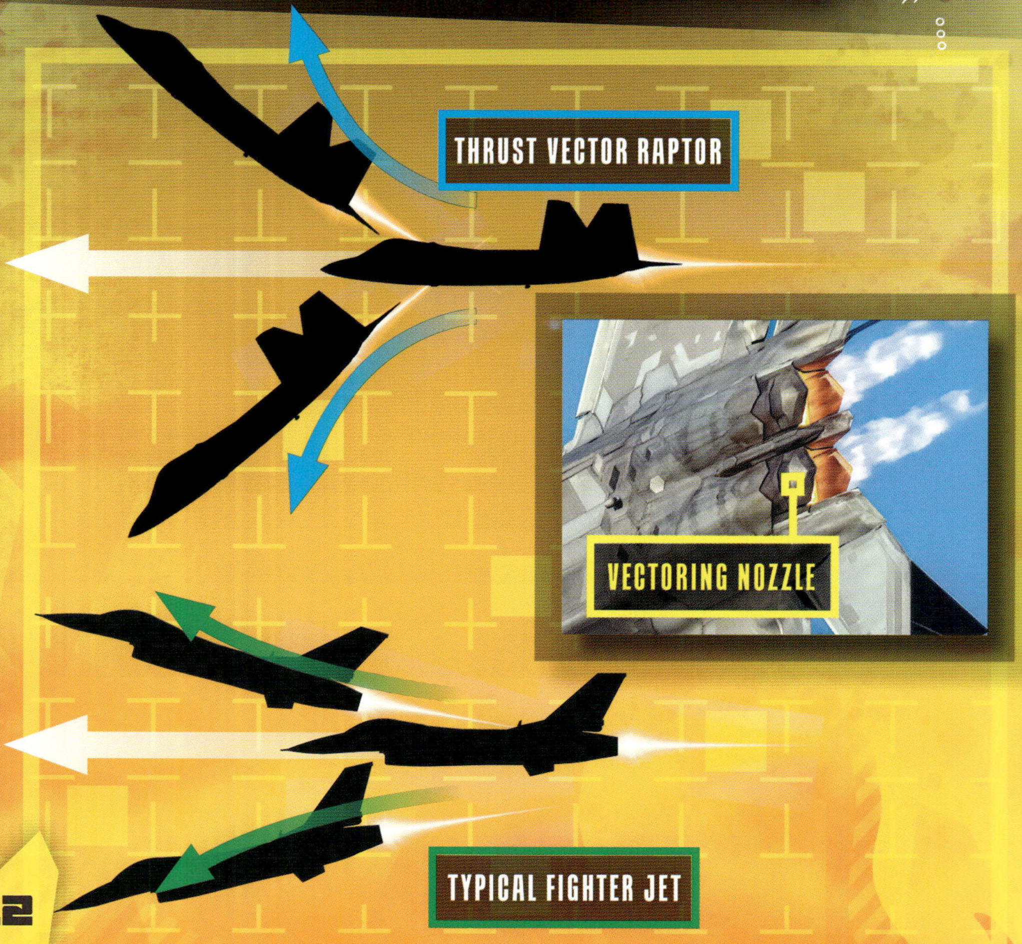

THRUST VECTOR RAPTOR

VECTORING NOZZLE

TYPICAL FIGHTER JET

FAST ON LESS!

The Raptor's engines use less fuel to reach supersonic speeds than any other aircraft.

The Raptor's engines are more powerful than other fighter jet engines. Its strong engines let the Raptor fly at supersonic speeds without using the afterburner. This is called **supercruise**.

MISSILE

The Raptor can carry many kinds of **missiles**. They are used to fight enemies in the air or on the ground. It also carries a **cannon**. It can fire up to 480 rounds.

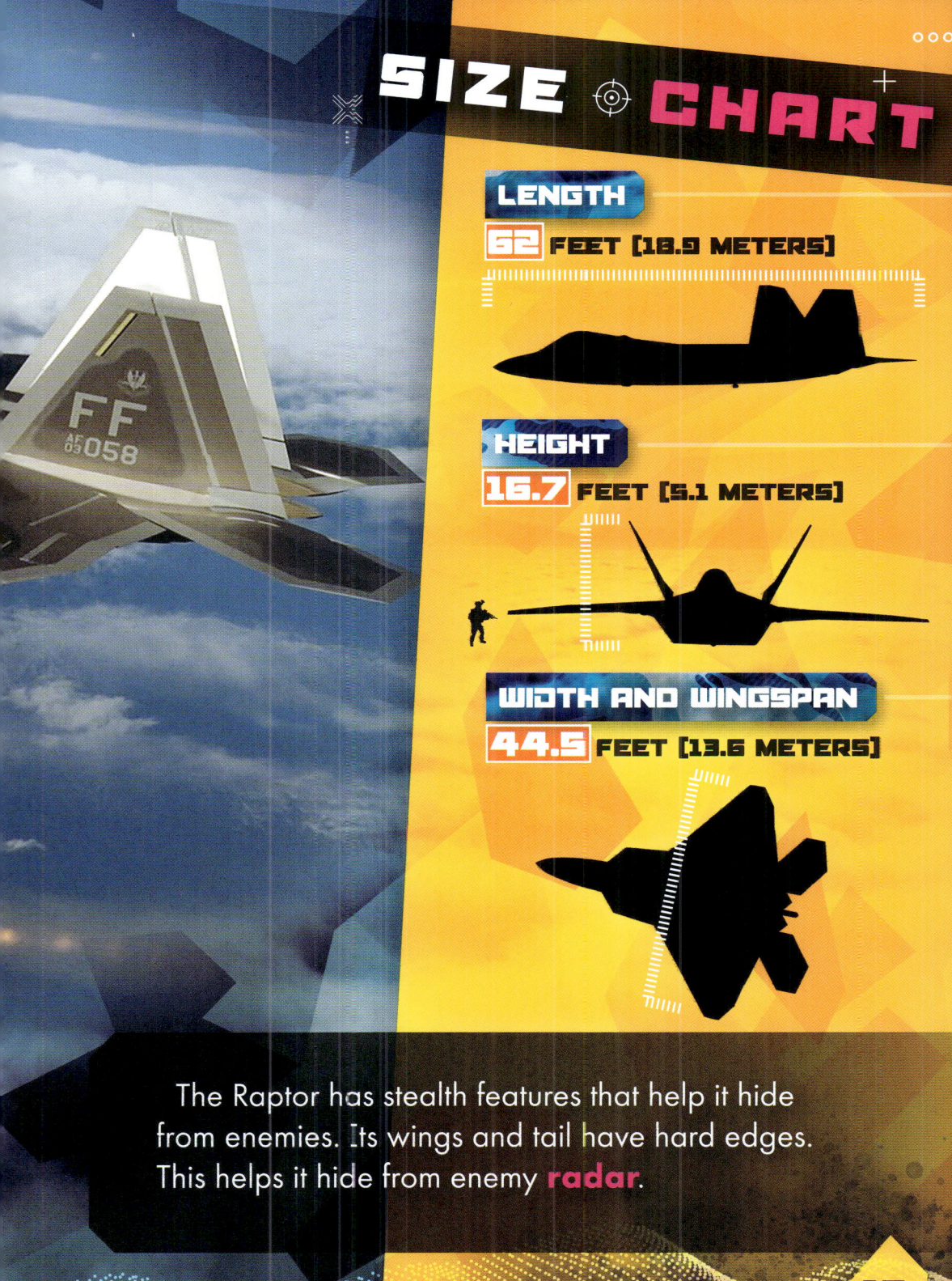

SIZE CHART

LENGTH
62 FEET (18.9 METERS)

HEIGHT
16.7 FEET (5.1 METERS)

WIDTH AND WINGSPAN
44.5 FEET (13.6 METERS)

The Raptor has stealth features that help it hide from enemies. Its wings and tail have hard edges. This helps it hide from enemy **radar**.

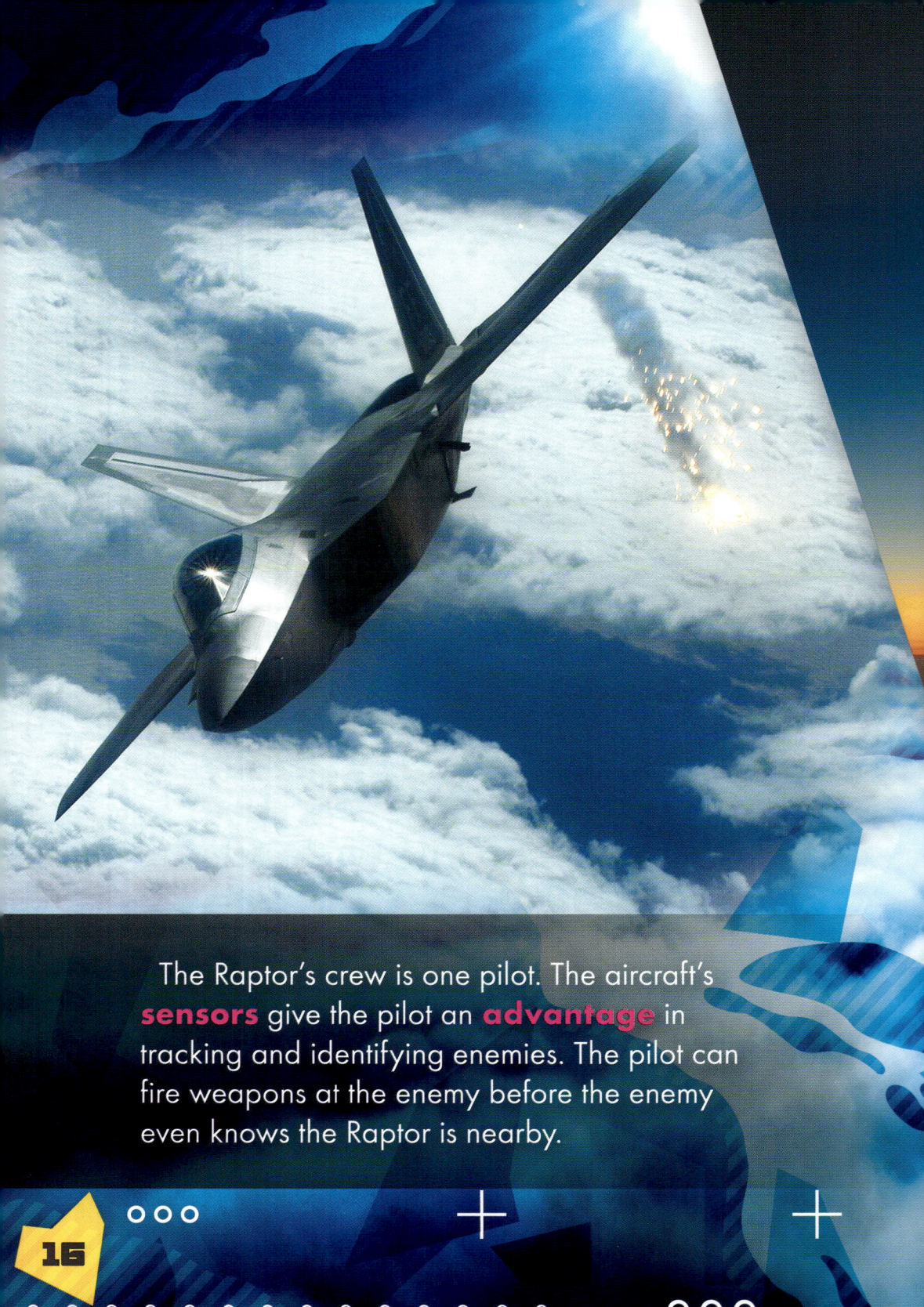

The Raptor's crew is one pilot. The aircraft's **sensors** give the pilot an **advantage** in tracking and identifying enemies. The pilot can fire weapons at the enemy before the enemy even knows the Raptor is nearby.

The pilot's helmet is equipped with night-vision goggles. They allow the pilot to see enemies even in the dark.

HELMET

THE RAPTOR'S FUTURE

The Raptor has only been needed in combat a few times. But it has helped the Air Force see and collect information about enemies.

The Air Force stopped making new Raptors in 2011. But they expect to keep flying the Raptors into the 2030s. Meanwhile, plans are underway for building the next Air Force fighter. More combat-ready jets are on the way!

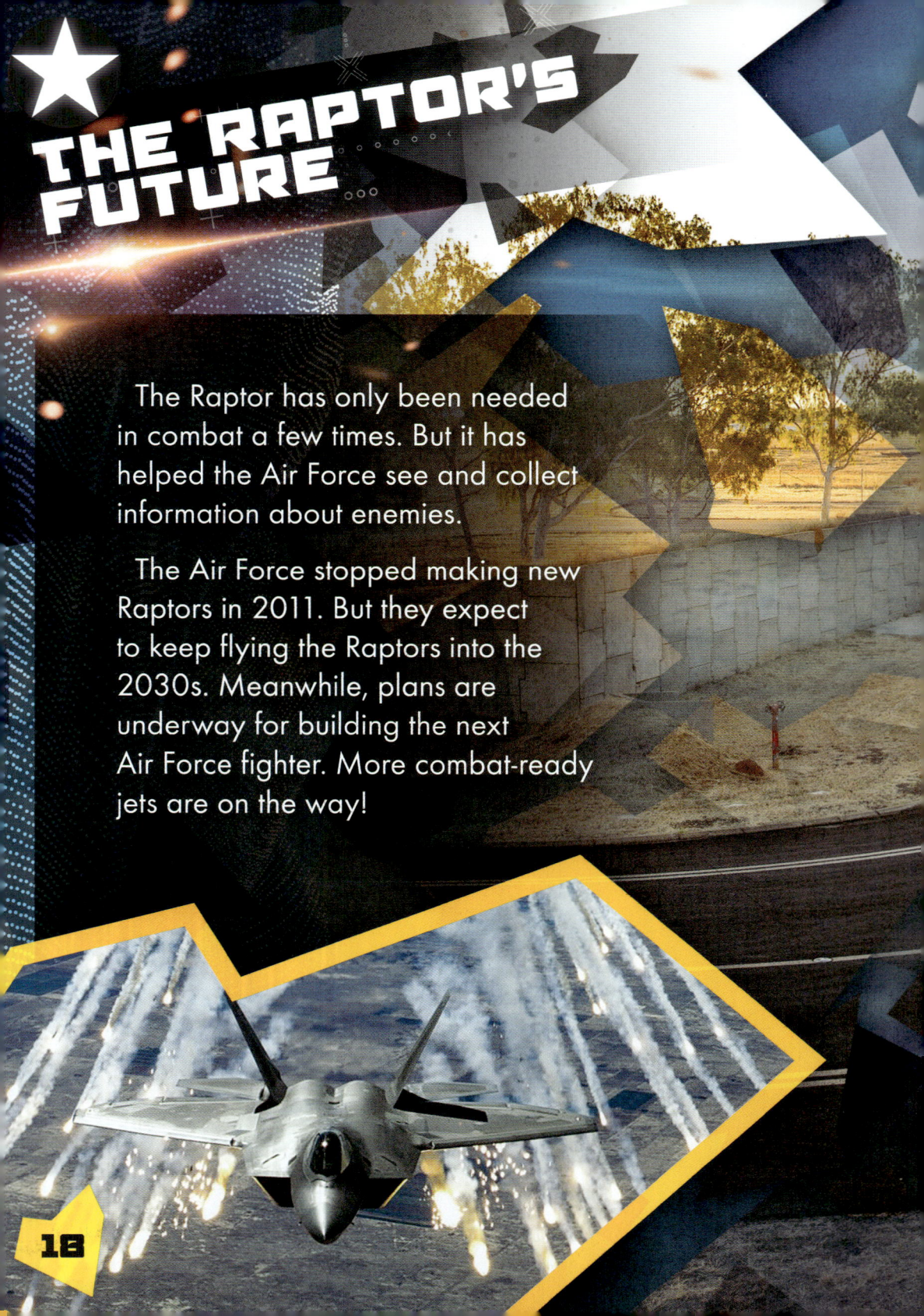

F-22 RAPTOR FACTS

STATS

TOP SPEED
1,535 miles (2,470 kilometers) per hour

RANGE
more than 1,850 miles (2,977 kilometers)

ALTITUDE CEILING
above 50,000 feet (15,240 meters)

WEAPONS

6 MISSILES

OR

2 BOMBS

100 100 80 100 100 — **480** CANNON ROUNDS

CLASS
STEALTH FIGHTER

CREW
1

OPERATION
OVER **183** F-22 RAPTORS IN USE TODAY

MANUFACTURERS
Lockheed Martin

AND

Boeing

BRANCH OF THE MILITARY
U.S. Air Force

MAIN PURPOSE
multi-role fighter

FIRST YEAR USED
1997

GLOSSARY

advantage—having a better chance of success

afterburner—a device on a jet engine that can boost its speed

agile—able to move quickly and easily

cannon—a large gun

cockpit—the part of an aircraft where the crew sits

combat—a fight between armed forces

missiles—explosives that are sent to targets

radar—a device that uses energy waves to sense and see objects

sensors—devices that detect objects and send that information to computers or other devices

stealth—related to being designed to avoid being seen

supercruise—to fly at supersonic speeds without needing an afterburner

supersonic—traveling faster than the speed of sound

thrust vectoring—the ability to move the angle of an engine to help an aircraft make sharper turns in the air

TO LEARN MORE

AT THE LIBRARY

Colson, Rob. *Awesome Aircraft*. New York, N.Y.: Enslow Publishing, 2023.

McKinney, Donna. *B-2 Stealth Bomber*. Minneapolis, Minn.: Bellwether Media, 2024.

Schuh, Mari. *Military Aircraft*. North Mankato, Minn.: Pebble, 2022.

ON THE WEB

Factsurfer.com gives you a safe, fun way to find more information.

1. Go to www.factsurfer.com

2. Enter "F-22 Raptor" into the search box and click 🔍.

3. Select your book cover to see a list of related content.

INDEX

afterburner, 5, 13
battle, 4, 6, 7
cannon, 14
cockpit, 4
combat, 9, 18
enemies, 4, 5, 6, 7, 10, 11, 14, 15, 16, 17, 18
engines, 5, 13
F-15 Eagle, 8
F-22 Raptor facts, 20–21
fuel, 13
future, 18
helmet, 17
history, 8, 9, 18
map, 9
missiles, 14
missions, 9
parts of an F-22 Raptor, 11
pilot, 4, 5, 16, 17
radar, 15
sensors, 16
size, 15

speed, 5, 6, 12, 13
spying, 7, 9
stealth technology, 6, 15
supercruise, 13
Syria, 9
tail, 15
thrust vectoring, 12
United States, 9, 11
United States Air Force, 6, 8, 10, 18
weapons, 6, 14, 16
wings, 15

The images in this book are reproduced through the courtesy of: Jason Robertson/ DVIDS, cover; Tiffany Emery/ DVIDS, pp. 3, 4; BlueBarronPhoto, p. 5; Joseph Leveille/ DVIDS, p. 6; Christine Del Aguila/ DVIDS, p. 7; Peter Brauns/ Alamy, p. 8; Aditya0635, pp. 10, 11 (top), 13; Eugene Berman, p. 11 (bottom); A. Michael Brown, p. 12; US Air Force/ Wikimedia Commons, p. 14 (missiles); Combat Archer/ Wikimedia Commons, p. 15; Clay Lancaster/ Wikimedia Commons, p. 16; Betty Chevalier/ DVIDS, p. 17; Samuel King Jr./ DVIDS, p. 17 (helmet); Ben Bloker/ Wikimedia Commons, p. 18; Robert Dabbs/ DVIDS, p. 19; Jerreht Harris/ DVIDS, p. 20; Nicholas J. De La Pena/ DVIDS, p. 23.